Animals in Houses and Gardens

ANIMALS

in

HOUSES AND GARDENS

RAINTREE PUBLISHERS
Milwaukee

This book has been reviewed
for accuracy by
Dr. Charles P. Milne, Jr.
Visiting Assistant Professor
Department of Biology
Marquette University, Milwaukee, Wisconsin

Copyright © 1988, Raintree Publishers Inc.

© 1986 Hachette, translated by Alison Taurel.

Library of Congress Number: 87-20775

  2 3 4 5 6 7 8 9 0   93 92 91 90 89

Printed and bound in the United States of America.

Library of Congress Cataloging in Publication Data

Animaux des maisons et des jardins. English.
  Animals in houses and gardens.

  Includes index.
  Summary: Describes mice, snails, flies, birds,
worms, spiders, cats, and other animals commonly
found in homes and gardens.
  1. Household ecology—Juvenile literature.
2. Garden fauna—Juvenile literature. 3. Animals—
Miscellanea—Juvenile literature. [1. Garden
animals] I. Title.
QH541.5.H67A5513 1987   591   87-20775
ISBN 0-8172-3114-5 (lib. bdg.)

CONTENTS

THE HOUSE MOUSE

THE ANCIENT HOUSE MOUSE

Mouse is a name given to many small kinds of rodents. There are hundreds of kinds of mice, and they live in most parts of the world. The house mouse is probably the best known kind of mouse. It is believed to have originally lived in ancient Asia. The name "mouse" comes from an old Sanskrit word meaning thief. Sanskrit is an ancient language of Asia.

Like rats, the house mouse spread from Asia to Europe and eventually other parts of the world. Descendents of this mouse now live in both North and South America. They were brought there by the ships of English, French and Spanish explorers.

The house mouse's color varies from gray to brown on its back and sides. Its stomach is often yellow-white. The mouse's coloring depends on whether it lives in a house or in the woods and fields. Most often the fur is soft and short. Short hairs or scaly skin also cover its long, slender tail.

The mouse has a small head and a pointed snout. Long, thin, mustache-like whiskers, like those of the cat, grow from the snout. These whiskers help the mouse feel its way about in the darkness. This is important because the mouse does not see well. Its small, dark eyes are weak, but its hearing and sense of smell are sharp.

All mice (like all rodents) have chisel-like front teeth. The mouse uses its teeth for gnawing. A rodent's teeth grow throughout its life. Gnawing keeps them short.

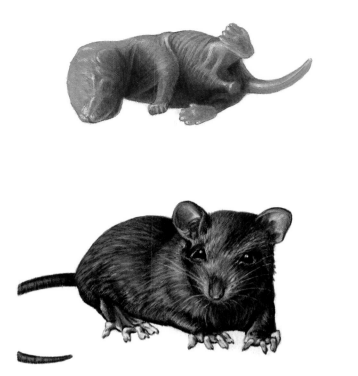

In a few weeks the baby mice become adults and are ready to reproduce.

Mice have long, arched front teeth called incisors. They grow throughout the rodent's life.

LIVING IN THE SHADOW

House mice live wherever they find food and shelter. Despite the name, some house mice actually live in the fields and woods. They dig holes in the ground and build nests of grass. But many other mice live near people. They nest in homes, garages and barns, choosing warm, dark spots for their nests.

Mice reproduce very quickly. A female may have four to eight litters, or groups of young, in a single year. The female carries her young in her body for about three weeks before they are born. She usually has between four and seven babies at a time. Newborn mice are helpless. They are born without fur and with their eyes closed. The female nurses the pink-colored babies for about three weeks after birth. By that time, their eyes are open and their fur has grown.

Mice do not store food like some rodents. Instead, they come out each night and eat whatever they can find. Mice are not fussy eaters. They eat almost anything: grain, vegetables, meats. They do not actually eat very much, but they gnaw on everything. House mice in the wild eat many of the same things. But food in the wild can be harder to find. These house mice must also depend on insects, leaves and roots for their food.

ALWAYS ON THE RUN

In the wild, mice live in constant danger. Dogs, cats, foxes, snakes, owls, hawks and most meat-eating animals prey on them. Even rats attack mice. Because of this, mice do not usually live very long. Few live longer than two or three months. In a house, a mouse may live a year or longer. But living among people is just as dangerous. People are probably the worst enemy of the mouse. Though the mice don't eat much, they do a lot of damage. They gnaw on books, boxes and all sorts of things, destroy food, and will over-run a house in a short time if left alone.

Despite the trouble it causes, the mouse can be useful. When domesticated, or tamed, mice make good pets. Mice, like rats, are also used in laboratory experiments and research projects. Using mice, scientists can learn about diseases, test new drugs, and study behavior. Their findings often help many people because researchers can perform experiments with mice that cannot be done on humans.

Although they don't eat much, mice can cause a lot of trouble. They gnaw on things, destroy food, and will overrun a house if left alone. A cat in the house is one way to control the mouse population. Cats are among the mouse's many predators.

THE SMALL GRAY SNAIL

A SHELL AND SOME HORNS

Down the garden path comes a snail. Its brown shell sits high on its back. Part of the snail's soft body sticks out of the shell. This is called the foot. The snail uses this strong, muscular organ to crawl. The snail's head can also be seen. It has four small "horns" sticking out of it. The snail seems to use the two smaller horns to feel its way along. These "horns," or tentacles, are long, flexible projections like those of the octopus. The two long upper ones end in dark spots that are the snail's eyes. Below these feelers is the snail's mouth. It is a small, half-moon opening.

Snails are found in many parts of the world — in jungles, oceans, lakes, deserts, forests, and in both warm and cold regions. There are more than 80,000 kinds of snails. Some are as small as a pinhead. Others can grow to two feet in length. Snails can live from two to twenty years. All snails can be divided into three groups: land snails, freshwater snails and saltwater snails. Where a snail lives determines its group.

THE LAND SNAIL

The gray snail is a land snail. Like earthworms, land snails are hermaphrodites. That means they have both male and female reproductive organs in their bodies. Even so, it still takes two snails to reproduce. Snails mate during the humid days of May and June. Mating sometimes takes several hours. Later, both snails will lay clusters of small, rubbery eggs in shallow holes in the ground. In a month the eggs will hatch, and small snails with transparent shells come out. Newborn snails are less than a quarter of an inch long.

The gray snail eats only vegetables, often dining on rotting plants. In gardens, it often eats lettuce, cabbages and carrots. The snail eats by tearing its food with its tongue.

A DAMP HOME

Snails prefer dampness. They often come out in large numbers when it rains. The rest of the time they hide in sheltered areas such as shady parks and gardens, under logs and stones, and in the woods. A few species even live in the deserts.

Sometimes snails cannot find as much moisture as they need. During these dry spells, they become dormant, or inactive. They draw back into their shells and seal the opening with a "door" of sticky liquid, or mucus. This door is called an epiphragm. It protects the snail from dry summers and harsh winters. When the outside air becomes moist again, the snails come out of their shells.

AT A SNAIL'S PACE

The snail is known to be a very slow-moving animal. It moves at a pace of about sixteen feet an hour. Because of

The snail eats by tearing food with its tongue.

One month after the snails mate, the eggs hatch underground.

A snail breeding container: 1) water opening, 2) air opening.

With a rippling motion, the snail moves on any surface.

its slow speed, the snail cannot run away from its enemies. It often gets crushed or eaten. The snail moves by the power of its foot. The muscles of the foot move backward in a wave-like motion that pushes the snail forward. As it moves, the snail squirts a sticky liquid, or mucus, from a gland under its head. This mucus leaves a shiny trail behind it. It lets the animal slip along easily and protects it from injury. A snail can even pass over glass and sharp stones without getting hurt.

USEFUL AND HARMFUL SNAILS

Most snails are harmless. They are an important food for fish and birds. Many people eat snails, too. They consider snails, or escargot as they are called, to be a delicacy. Some people even collect live snails after a rainfall and try to prepare them on their own. In many places, collecting snails is forbidden. Some snails are rare and protected by law. Even where snail collecting is allowed, people should be careful. Some snails can be harmful if eaten. Those living near polluted waters or sewers should be avoided. These snails can carry diseases such as typhoid and hepatitis.

Snails can also be harmful for other reasons. Some land snails do much damage to crops. Farmers consider the giant African snail a serious pest. It destroys flowers, vegetables and young rubber tree plants.

THE FLY

TROUBLESOME TWO WINGS

People think of flies as small drab-colored insects. A closer look, however, shows that some flies are much more colorful. Some flies shine a metallic blue or green color, or have orange, yellow or white markings. Flies come in many shapes, sizes and colors. There are about 150,000 different kinds, or species, of flies throughout the world.

The one thing all flies have in common is their wings. All true flies have two wings. This is easy to remember if you know the fly's scientific name, Diptera. Diptera comes from Greek words meaning "two wings." True flies include familiar insects such as the housefly, the fruit fly, the horsefly, the mosquito and the tsetse fly.

A THREE-PART BODY

The fly, like all insects, has three main parts to its body. The first part is the large head with its two huge eyes. The fly's eyes cover most of its head. Some flies have such large eyes that they actually touch each other. The fly has compound eyes. This means its eyes have many facets, or lenses. With its compound eyes, the fly can see in many directions at once. It can see any movement quickly.

The fly's mouth is a straw-like part called the proboscis. It is used for sucking liquid, which is the fly's only food. Certain flies, like black flies, horseflies and mosquitos, seem to bite. A "biting" fly actually stabs its victim with its proboscis. It then injects its saliva into the wound to prevent the blood from clotting. The fly is then free to suck the victim's blood.

The middle part of the fly's body is called the thorax. The insect's legs and wings are attached here. A fly has six jointed legs which usually end in claws and hairy pads, called pulvilli. Both help the fly cling to flat surfaces like walls, ceilings or even glass. The fly's wings are thin and veined. Behind them are two small knobbed structures called halteres. These give the fly balance in flight. Flies are among the fastest of all flying insects. The familiar buzz of the fly is actually the sound of its wings beating. The housefly's wings beat about 200 times per second.

The last part of the fly's body is the abdomen. Air enters the fly through holes, called spiracles, along the sides of its body. The abdomen has eight pairs of spiracles. The thorax has two pairs. The abdomen houses the digestive system and reproductive organs.

PART OF THE LIFE CYCLE

Most flies reproduce quickly and in large numbers. Some females lay from 1 to 250 yellowish eggs at a time. The eggs are often laid in decaying matter, such as dead animals or garbage, or in animal waste. The eggs quickly hatch worm-like larvae, called maggots. The larvae feed on the matter in which they were laid. The larvae shed their skins,

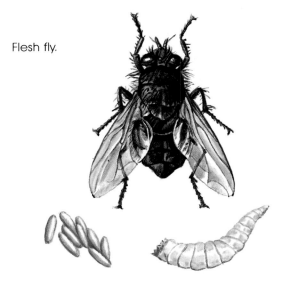

Flesh fly.

The fly eggs quickly hatch, giving birth to larvae called maggots.

A green blow fly.

A housefly.

The fly's two, large, faceted eyes allow it to see in many directions at one time.

or molt, several times before becoming pupae. In the hard, brownish shell, or puparium, of the pupae, the adult fly develops. When they are fully grown, the flies burst from the shell and crawl out. Adult flies do not grow as they get older. Houseflies live about thirty days in the summer. Many of them will die when the weather gets cold. However, some larvae and pupae do live through the winter. These become adults in the spring.

Flies can be helpful. Because they feed on decaying matter and garbage, they are very important to the life cycle. Other flies carry pollen from plant to plant, just like bees, or feed on harmful insects. Still other flies, such as the fruit fly, are studied by scientists. From these studies, they learn how certain traits, or characteristics, are passed from generation to generation.

Still, flies are pests. Even when they are not biting or buzzing, their presence is bothersome. Some people say that a half lemon stuck with cloves will keep the flies away. But the worst thing about flies is that they are germ carriers. They carry germs both in their bodies and in the hair on their bodies. These germs can cause diseases such as malaria, sleeping sickness, and typhoid. The fly spreads its germs to anything it touches or bites.

THE GREAT TIT

A FAMILIAR ACROBAT

The great tit is a familiar bird in many European gardens. It is easy to recognize with its black head and white cheeks. Black feathers also cover the bird's neck, and a stripe of black runs down its bright yellow belly.

Tit, or titmouse, is the name for a number of small, friendly birds. The titmouse is known for its long, soft feathers. It lives mainly in the warmer parts of Europe, North America and Africa and is related to the nuthatch. The black-capped chickadee is the most common North American titmouse, and the tufted titmouse is the largest. The tufted titmouse gets its name from the high, gray tuft of feathers that stand at the top of its head.

The great tit is the largest European titmouse. It is about the same size as the tufted titmouse. The great tit is a quick, active bird, and it is not timid. While looking for food, it explores even the thinnest branches. Because of this, the tit sometimes finds itself hanging upside down. Luckily, its feet have a strong grip. The bird hunts comfortably while hanging upside down from bark, a small twig, or a flexible stem.

CHOOSING A NESTING SPOT

The great tit is a cave-loving bird. It often builds its home in holes in trees, in cracks in walls, and under roofs.

Sometimes it chooses to nest in places such as mailboxes, pipes, bricks, or other birds' old nests. Many people know that the great tit will nest in almost anything cave-like. They build nests for the bird and hope that it will nest near them. Building nests for the titmouse gives people the chance to watch the bird.

If titmice are found in your area, you might also try this. Flower pots make great nests for titmice. Simply cover the pot's open end with a small board. The board can be held in place with wire. Also be sure to check the small hole at the other end of the pot. It should be about an inch (three centimeters) wide for a titmouse nest. A larger or smaller hole will attract different kinds of birds. If it is too small, you can make it bigger with a file. Then all you have to do is hang the nest on the wall of a garage or other building.

BUILDING THE NEST

The female great tit is the nest builder. She chooses her nesting spot early in the year. But she does not actually begin the work until she is nearly ready to lay her eggs. The building then begins sometime in March. The male titmouse will sometimes help, gathering building material for the female. The nest is built low to the ground with twigs, roots and grass. It is lined with

A fourteen-day-old chick. Titmouse chicks stay in the nest for two to three weeks.

moss, roots, down and animal fur. In the nest, the bird lays from eight to thirteen rust-flecked eggs. She then broods for about two weeks. Brood means to sit on and keep warm. At birth, the chicks are covered with gray down. They stay in the nest for about two to three weeks. Females often lay two clutches, or nests of eggs, a year.

A HARDY, INDEPENDENT BIRD

The great tit has a short, powerful beak and a tough crop. A crop is a pouch in a bird's throat where food digestion begins. The tit's beak and crop allow it to eat more than just insects and spiders. For example, the tit can eat hairy caterpillars that many other birds avoid.

The tit is a hardy bird. This is important during the winter when many kinds of food are hard to find. Then the tit eats insects and larvae that are still alive, food scraps, seeds and berries. It is also fond of fats. Because the tit is a hardy bird, it adapts to the diet change.

The titmouse sets up its nest in the cavities of old walls.

THE EARTHWORM

THE NIGHT CRAWLER

Many people know the earthworm by its nickname night crawler. The earthworm is a common worm found in the moist soil of warm regions throughout the world. It can often be found in the garden soil. There, a single shovel-scoop brings a handful or more of worms to the surface. On damp nights, especially after a rain, earthworms come from their tunnels. With a flashlight they can be seen in the grass. Hundreds lie partially hidden in their holes, ready to disappear into the earth in a moment.

Earthworms have long, thin, pink or red-brown bodies. They vary in size from 1/25 of an inch to almost eleven feet long. The average worm is about seven inches long. The earthworm has a very simple brain. It has no eyes or ears, but it is very sensitive to heat, light and touch.

The worm's skin is bare and smooth. This helps it move easily along the ground or in the soil. The skin is marked by many rings or segments, called annuli. Each segment is actually a muscle. The worm crawls by lengthening and shortening these muscles like a coil. It pushes through the soil with its front part. It then grabs onto the earth and pulls up the rear part. Small hairs or bristles, called setae, help the worm control its movements. These hairs are found in pairs along the worm's underside. They help the worm move forward and can also keep it from slipping.

The earthworm has no lungs. It breathes through its skin from air pockets in the soil. When it rains, the air spaces fill with water. The earthworm could drown. This is why many earthworms leave their tunnels when it rains. The worm must also avoid very hot, dry places. Too much heat may dry the worm's skin. This will also kill it.

A HARD-WORKING WORM

Gardeners and farmers consider the earthworm a very important animal. Its tunnels bring air and rainwater into the soil's deep layers. Plants need both air and water to grow. The earthworm's tunnels bring these things to them.

The earthworm is also useful because it feeds on decaying (dead) plants in the soil. It eats huge amounts of earth each day. When it is young, it may take in thirty times its weight. Later it takes in less — perhaps only ten times its weight. Some of the earth is digested. The rest is excreted, or given off, back into the earth. As excrement, the soil has been mixed with the worm's bodily juices. It is now finer and more fertile than it was. Plants do better in this new soil. Mixing the soil is the earthworm's most important

The earthworm farm.

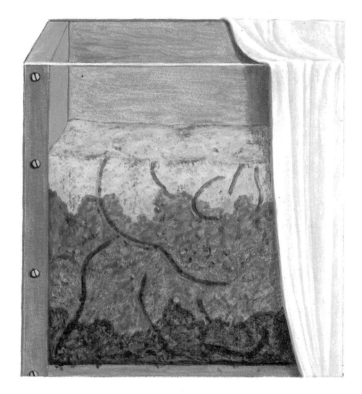

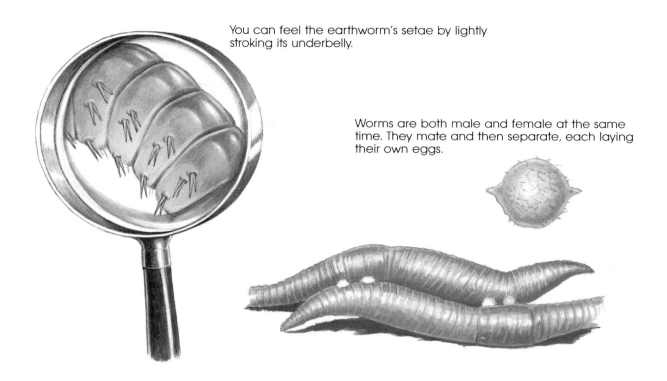

You can feel the earthworm's setae by lightly stroking its underbelly.

Worms are both male and female at the same time. They mate and then separate, each laying their own eggs.

function. Like the mole, the earthworm brings some soil elements to the surface and drags others back down to the deep layers.

AND COUNTLESS, TOO

The work of one earthworm alone would not change the soil much. But there are many, many earthworms in a single acre of land. Some people say that this is because of the way the worms reproduce. They say that when a worm is cut in two, two worms are born. Worms do reproduce quickly, but that is not the way they do it. Earthworms, like snails, are hermaphrodites. That means they have both male and female reproductive organs in their bodies. However, to reproduce, each worm must mate with another.

Only then can eggs form. After mating, both worms lay eggs. The eggs hatch in several weeks.

AN EARTHWORM FARM

You can see the earthworm's effects on soil by building an earthworm farm. An earthworm farm is a small, narrow cage with transparent (see through) walls. Fill the cage with several different-colored types of earth. These should be laid in horizontal layers. Cover the soil with dead leaves and moisten it. Add a dozen earthworms to the cage. Finally, cover the cage with a black cloth and put it in the basement. Each day you will be able to see how the different soils are mixed. The earthworm does the same thing to the earth.

THE LADYBUG

A BEETLE OF A DIFFERENT COLOR

Everyone knows the ladybug. The ladybug, with its bright red body and black spots is certainly a familiar insect. Often called a ladybird, it is any of about 5,000 kinds of small, round beetles. It is often red or yellow with black spots. But other color combinations are possible. The ladybug's coloring depends on what kind of ladybug it is. The same is true for the number of spots the insect has. There are ladybugs with ten, fourteen and even twenty-four spots. Those with seven or two spots are the most common.

THE LADYBUG

Although ladybugs have many different wing patterns, their bodies are the same. Ladybugs commonly have small heads and pea-shaped bodies with short legs. They also have two sets of wings. A larger outer set of wings hides a smaller set of wings beneath it. The outer wings, called elytra, make up the ladybug's colorful "shell." They protect the smaller, transparent wings when the ladybug is not flying. The bright wings also warn ladybug predators, such as birds and spiders. When attacked, ladybugs sometimes squirt a yellow-orange liquid (blood) from their legs. The liquid smells bad and leaves a bad taste. A predator who has tasted a ladybug will remember the bitter taste. It probably will not attack a ladybug again.

The ladybug lays bright yellow eggs in small packets of about fifteen. The ladybug usually hides its eggs under leaves or bark. After about twelve days, larvae hatch from the eggs. The larvae are long and thin. Most often they are a gray color with bright or pale spots. The larvae do not look much like the familiar ladybug. But they soon will. Like most insects, the ladybug larvae go through a process of change, called metamorphosis. At the end of this time, they become the ladybug adult that people know. Adult ladybugs live a little more than a year.

The ladybug lays eggs grouped in packets of fifteen.

The ladybug larva looks very different than the full-grown insect.

THE BOLD, BEAUTIFUL LADYBUG

People consider the ladybug a pleasant insect. It is small and brightly colored. It does not sting or bite. It can easily be caught and held. The ladybug's relatives such as the grasshopper, the wasp, the fly and the mosquito are not always as friendly.

However, in its own world, the ladybug is a fierce hunter with a huge appetite. Most ladybugs are insectivorous. This means they eat other insects. The ladybug is very fond of the tiny, plant-sucking aphid. It wanders about on

1) A ladybug with twenty-two spots.   2) A ladybug with five spots.

People consider the ladybug a friendly insect. It does not bite or sting.

plant leaves searching for these and other plant pests.

For this reason, the ladybug is thought of as a very helpful insect. Farmers discovered its importance in the Middle Ages. They considered the ladybug sacred. Its reputation has continued to grow. During the 1900s, the cottony-cushion scale insect nearly destroyed the California orange crop. Ladybugs were brought in from Australia to eat the pests. They saved the crop. Even today, ladybugs are often placed in areas where there are large pest populations. Many people consider them good luck.

FINDING A WINTER HOME

Many insects die before winter. Others spend the time as an egg or pupa. The ladybug lives through the winter as an adult. Before the cold weather comes, hundreds and thousands of ladybugs gather together. They find a shelter under dead leaves or in cracks around tree trunks and crawl in. In the shelter, the ladybugs "sleep," or hibernate, for the winter. Because they do not move around, the ladybugs need very little energy. They live on the food stored in their bodies. But it is still not known why so many ladybugs hibernate in the same place. When the spring comes, the ladybugs will go their separate ways once more.

THE HOUSE MARTIN

RELATIVE OF
THE SWALLOW

Martin is the name for several types of small birds. The martin is a member of the swallow family. Generally, this family of birds is known for its graceful flight and slim, streamlined form. The martin is said to be streamlined because its body is well-suited for life in the air. The swallow family also has tiny feet, long pointed wings and short bills. They are found throughout the world.

The house martin is a European martin. It is slightly smaller than its American cousin, the purple martin. The purple martin is the largest North American swallow. The house martin is easily spotted by the white mark over its lower back. This white patch cuts through the dark color of the rest of the bird's tail, back and wings. This same white covers most of the bird's underside. Seen from below, the martin seems to be a white bird. The martin is also known by its slightly V-shaped tail.

The martin is a lively, nervous bird that does not stay long in one spot. It usually lives in small groups, or colonies. Many of the colonies are built right in the city, very near people. The martin returns to the same nesting spot each year and begins building a nest immediately. The large nest must be finished quickly. The martin chicks must be raised and on their own by September. At that time, the martins will begin to move, or migrate, south for the winter.

BUILDER OF NESTS

After the martins arrive in the north, the male of each pair chooses a spot for the nest. The house martins are known for their nests. They are often seen hanging from under the eaves of buildings. A window ledge or other sheltered spot is also often used. The nests are built of small pellets of mud. The martins gather the dirt from the ground. When mixed with the birds' saliva, the dirt makes an excellent mortar, or paste. It hardens when it dries. With the mortar, the martins build a bulky, half-sphere nest. A small, round opening on the upper side is their door.

When the nest is finished, the martins line the inside with grass, feathers and other soft materials. The female then lays four or five eggs. She broods on the nest for fifteen to sixteen days. The male sometimes takes a turn. Occasionally, the female martin will lay a second set of eggs. But everything must be done quickly. The young must be ready to migrate by summer's end.

At birth, the house martin chicks are born with their eyes closed. They are covered with a soft down.

Perched on telephone wires, the house martin 1) sometimes meets its relative, the chimney swallow 2).

A WELCOMED VISITOR

The house martin, like many martins and swallows, is a welcome visitor in many places. The colonies can sometimes be noisy, but the martin is a big insect eater. Ants, flies, beetles and especially mosquitos are all favorites of the martin.

Because of this, people encourage martins to nest near their homes. Many swallows have left their cliffs and hollows for man-made nesting sites. The purple martin once nested under rocks. They now live in the cities in highrise apartments built for them. These apartment houses stand on large poles and have room for twenty or more martin pairs.

A WINTER TRAVELLER

In September, migration begins. The entire house martin population leaves its summer nesting spot and flies south. In good weather, the martins fly six or eight hours a day, at speeds of about eighteen to twenty-five miles an hour. In getting to their winter homes, the martins face many dangers. Extreme weather conditions may kill them. Larger birds may prey on the passing flock. Somehow the martins survive these things, only to begin the whole journey again in the spring.

When bird-watching, it is best to stay far enough away so as not to disturb the birds. A pair of binoculars makes it possible to get a close-up view while still at a distance.

THE MOLE

AN UNDERGROUND LIFE

Moles are small, thick-bodied mammals. They spend most of their lives underground, tunneling through the soil. A common North American mole is the star-nosed mole. Its name comes from the fringe of naked, fleshy feelers around its nose. Moles are also found in Europe and Asia. These moles may look slightly different than North American moles. But the animals' habits are very much alike.

BUILT FOR DIGGING

The mole's round, or cylindrical, body is made for digging and living underground. Its short black or gray fur is very dense and protects the mole from what might seem a dirty, dusty life. The fur also lies in whichever direction it is brushed. This makes it easy for the mole to scurry back and forth in its tunnels. The mole's head is wedge-shaped and ends in a pointed pink snout. The snout, which is very sensitive, helps guide the mole.

The mole has four short legs. The front legs, or forelegs, end in five, finger-like claws. These forelegs are very powerful. The mole uses them like shovels to hollow out tunnels. The back legs are also strong, but they are shorter than those in front.

Hidden in the mole's fur are two tiny eyes. The animal is nearly blind, since it does not need sharp vision in its dark

The mole often tunnels near tree roots. Food is likely to be found there.

tunnels. Good ears and a sharp sense of smell supply the mole with information about its surroundings.

CASTLES IN THE LAWN

It is easy to tell when moles have moved into the neighborhood. The small mounds of earth that dot the yard or garden are a sure sign. These mounds are called molehills. The European mole is famous for its home. It looks like an underground fortress, or castle. The home has a central chamber or room attached to two round chambers. One tunnel, called the bolt run, is the mole's emergency exit. The others lead to feeding grounds. The mole builds a cozy nest of leaves and grass in one of the main chambers. This main nest is often built well below the earth's surface for protection. In early spring, the female mole will have two to seven young in it.

EARTHWORMS: A FAVORITE FOOD

The mole needs a lot of food. It uses its cutting teeth, called incisors, and sharp fangs to kill its prey. Scurrying through its tunnels, the mole hunts its favorite food — earthworms. It also feeds on grubs, caterpillars and insects. When there are many earthworms, the mole will gather and store them. Its stores are sometimes quite large. A mole hunting for food finds its prey by movement in the ground, or vibration. As it closes in on its prey, the mole's sense of smell guides it.

NEIGHBOR PROBLEMS

Having moles in the area can be useful. Moles help farmers by controlling insect populations that could hurt crops. Their tunnels, like the earthworm's, bring air and water to the plants. Their burrowing mixes the soil, making it richer and more fertile. Still, many people consider the mole a pest.

They are not pleased to find its castles in their lawns. The mole itself does not cause any damage. However, the mounds it leaves in gardens, lawns and golf courses are bothersome.

Getting rid of moles is not easy. It is as difficult to catch a mole as it is to see one. Many farmers put traps in the mole's tunnels. Planting certain flowers is also said to discourage the mole.

Years ago, people called on the mole catcher to get rid of the moles. Armed with traps, the mole catcher moved from farm to farm, offering his services. The moles he captured were skinned, and their small furs were sold for money.

The mole's young are born in one of the main chambers.

THE SPIDER

THE ARACHNID

Many people think spiders are insects. Scientists classify, or group, them under a different name. The spider belongs to a group known as arachnids. They are different than insects in several ways. For one thing, spiders have eight legs. Ants, beetles, bees and other insects have only six legs. Many insects also have wings and antennae (feelers), but spiders do not. Other arachnids include scorpions, mites and ticks.

Many people are afraid of spiders. But only hurt or frightened spiders bite people. Any very few spider bites are even harmful to people. In North America, only six spiders have dangerous bites. These are the brown recluse spider, the sack spider, the black widow, the brown widow, the red-legged widow, and the varied widow.

There are many species of spiders. Some are smaller than the head of a pin. Others, such as the South American tarantula, may grow as large as ten inches long. Most spiders are a dull brown, black or gray color. But some spiders are as brightly colored as butterflies. You can use a magnifying glass for a close inspection of a spider's color and markings. Without bothering it, make a sketch of it. Compare this sketch to others you find.

As different as the spider species can be, their body structures are a lot alike. The spider's body has two sections: the cephalothorax and the abdomen. The cephalothorax is made up of a joined head and middle body, or thorax. The spider's eight legs are attached here.

Each leg has several joints and ends in small claws. The abdomen is the large end body section.

IN THE SPIDER'S WEB

At the rear of the abdomen there are short, finger-like organs called spinnerets. The spider's silk comes from its spinnerets. Most spiders have six spinnerets. Some have as few as two. All spiders can spin silk, but not all spiders make webs. Still, silk is very important to all spiders. A spider uses its silk to spin a thin thread, or dragline, wherever it goes. As it moves, the spider attaches this dragline in different places. The dragline can help a spider escape from an enemy or feel the movement of prey in its web.

Spiders also use silk to build their nests. Each kind of spider builds its own type of nest. Many build the familiar web with its many lines and details. Some line a folded leaf with silk for a nest. Others have burrows in the ground lined with silk.

COURTSHIP AND MATING

As soon as male spiders mature, they look for mates. In most species, the female spider is bigger than the male. The female sometimes mistakes the male for prey and eats him. But most males perform a special mating dance. This helps the female "recognize" the male.

The female lays eggs several weeks or months after mating. The number of eggs can vary from one to several

By temporarily caging a spider, you can see it work before your eyes.

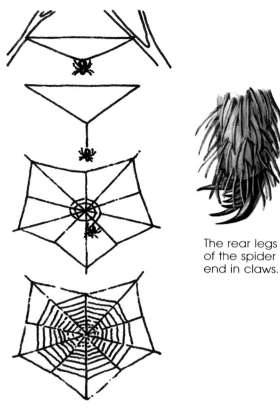

The steps in spinning a web.

The rear legs of the spider end in claws.

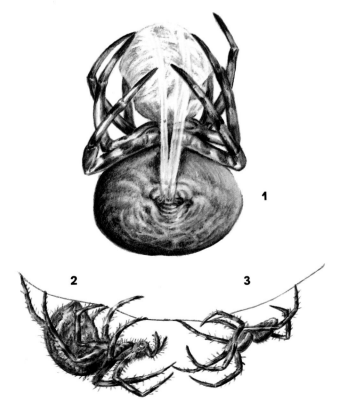

1) A thick liquid comes out of the spider's abdomen. When it dries, it becomes a silken thread.   2) The female.   3) The male.

thousand. Most females wrap their eggs in a silk case. This case is very strong and waterproof. In some species, the female dies after making the case. Other types of female spiders stay with their eggs until they hatch into young spiders, or spiderlings.

HUNTING AND SPINNING

Spiders can be divided into two main groups: hunters and web spinners. Hunting spiders actually hunt their prey. They have sharp eyes that can see insects far away. After spotting something, a hunting spider will chase it or wait to pounce on it. Some hunting spiders can jump very far.

Web spinners do not have sharp eyesight. They must depend on their webs to trap insects. The threads of the spider's web are sticky. Insects stick to the thread, but the spider does not. Its body is covered with an oil that keeps the thread from sticking to it.

Once a spider has trapped its prey, it uses its fangs to seize and kill it. All spiders have a pair of "fangs" or chelicerae. The chelicerae are found between the spider's eyes and mouth. Each ends in a hollow pointed claw. Poison is injected into the victim through these. This paralyzes or kills the spider's victim. Some spiders crush insects with their chelicerae. Still others use them to dig burrows for their nests.

THE CAT

A DOMESTIC FELINE

The cat, like the dog, is called a domestic animal. That means it has been tamed, or taught, to live with or near people. The cat was tamed several thousand years ago. It has been kept as a pet ever since. People sometimes forget that the cat belongs to the feline family. Among members of this family are the lion, tiger, leopard, jaguar, cheetah and puma.

There are many kinds of cats. But all cats are alike in certain ways. Cats are skilled hunters. With their quick, silent walk, they can sneak up on unsuspecting animals and pounce on them. Cats are generally nocturnal. That is, they are most active at night.

A SKILLED HUNTER

Cats are also carnivorous, or meat eating. House cats often prey on animals like mice or birds. Larger members of the feline family may prey on animals like antelopes and deer.

Most cats have long, narrow bodies and thick fur. The cat's hair can be long or short, depending on the species. They have long hind legs and powerful muscles. They can jump high and far and run very quickly. Cats also have sharp teeth and claws. Most cats can draw their claws back into their paws when they relax. Cats use their teeth and claws for hunting. With them, they can seize and kill their prey. Cats also use their claws for climbing.

A cat's sharp senses help it in its hunting. Cats have a sharp sense of hearing and smell. Their eyes are particularly strong. Cats can see better in dim light than people can. But cats cannot see in complete darkness. Cats whiskers are also very sensitive. Most cats have from twenty to thirty long whiskers in rows along the sides of their faces. The whiskers help the cat feel its way through bushes.

A DISTANT COMPANION

The domestic cat is a small member of the cat family. Although it is tame, it still has some of its wild relatives' traits, or qualities. Still, the cat is a popular house pet. For many people, the cat is a pleasant, clean and faithful companion. It is certainly one of the smartest of all tame animals and can be trained. But training a cat to do anything is often not as easy as training a dog. A cat often acts very independently. Then it ignores everyone and goes off on its own. The cat does not need people.

Cats live happily in the cities or country areas. But despite the way they act, many cats do need someone to care for them. They need to be clean, warm and dry. They depend on their owners for a warm place to live, food to eat and water to drink. In return, many cats help people. They kill rats and mice in homes, stores, warehouses, and farm

When she senses that her young are in danger, the mother cat moves the kittens to a safe place.

buildings. Cats have been doing this since ancient times. Scientists believe that the Egyptians probably tamed cats to live with people. They used them to keep rats and mice from overrunning their grain storehouses.

EVEN MORE DISTANT

Cats are even more private when having kittens. Most female cats begin mating by six months of age. They have their first litter by the time they are one or two years old. The mother cat carries her young in her body for about two months before they are born. Most cats mate in late winter or early spring. A female may have litters two to three times a year.

When the time comes, the mother cat chooses a dark, hidden place to have her young. It may choose the back of a closet, a laundry basket, a soft pile of hay, or any other cozy spot. The darkness protects the kittens' sensitive eyes. The privacy keeps them safe from any enemies. Even some male cats may hurt or kill the kittens. The kittens stay with their mother for about two months. She nurses them during the whole time.

Cats are full grown by the end of the first year. Females become adults slightly sooner than males. Most cats live for about fourteen years. Some have been known to live past thirty years.

FACTS AT A GLANCE

Scientific classification is a method of identifying and organizing all living things. Using this method, scientists place plants and animals in groups according to similar characteristics. Characteristics are traits or qualities that make one organism different from another.

There are seven major breakdowns, or groups, to this method of classification. They include: kingdom, phylum, class, order, family, genus, and species. The kingdom is the largest group. It contains the most kinds of animals or plants. For example, all animals belong to the animal kingdom, Animalia. The species is the smallest of the groupings. Members of a species are alike in many ways. They are also different from all other living things in one or more ways.

THE HOUSE MOUSE

Phylum:	**Chordata** (vertebrates)
Class:	**Mammalia** (mammals)
Order:	**Rodentia** (gnawing animals)
Size:	2½ to 4 inches long
Reproduction:	Between four and eight litters of 4 to 8 young per year
Habitat:	Houses, fields, bushes and woods in many parts of the world
Diet:	Grain, vegetables, meats, seeds, plants

THE SMALL GRAY SNAIL

Phylum:	**Mollusca** (soft-bodied)
Class:	**Gastropods** (single-valve or shell)
Order:	**Stylommatophora**
Size:	From less than inch to 2 feet long
Reproduction:	50 to 80 eggs per mating season
Habitat:	Damp, shady areas such as parks, gardens, woods, edges of ponds, rivers. Found on all continents.
Diet:	Plant parts, especially rotting matter

THE FLY

Phylum:	**Arthropoda** (joint-footed animals)
Class:	**Insecta** (insects)
Order:	**Diptera** (two-winged)
Size:	From 1/20 of an inch to 3 inches long
Reproduction:	1 to 250 eggs at a time; up to 1,000 a year. Four-stage metamorphosis (egg, maggot, pupa, adult)
Habitat:	Found in vicinity of people throughout the world
Diet:	Maggot — plant, animal or other matter Adult — liquids

THE GREAT TIT

Phylum:	**Chordata** (vertebrates)
Class:	**Aves** (birds)
Order:	**Passeriformes** (perching birds)
Size:	5½ inches long; wingspan of 8 to 9 inches
Reproduction:	One or two broods of 8 to 13 eggs per year
Habitat:	Forests, parks and gardens of Europe except for far north
Diet:	Insects, seeds, berries

THE EARTHWORM

Phylum:	**Annelida** (segmented worms)
Class:	**Oligochaeta** (few bristles)
Order:	**Terricole** (living in soil)
Size:	From 1/25 of an inch to 11 feet long; averages 7 inches
Reproduction:	Hermaphrodites (have both male and female reproductive organs) but must mate to reproduce. After mating, both worms lay eggs
Habitat:	Tunnels in moist soil. Found in warm regions throughout the world
Diet:	Decaying plant matter

THE HOUSE MARTIN

Phylum:	**Chordata** (vertebrates)
Class:	**Aves** (birds)
Order:	**Passeriformes** (perching birds)
Size:	6 to 7½ inches long
Reproduction:	One or two broods of 4 to 5 eggs per year
Habitat:	Cities throughout Europe in warmer weather; migrates to Africa for winters.
Diet:	Insects

THE SPIDER

Phylum:	**Arthropoda** (joint-footed animals)
Class:	**Arachnida**
Order:	**Araneae**
Size:	From less than an inch to 10 inches long
Reproduction:	An average of 100 eggs per mating season
Habitat:	Fields, woods, caves, swamps, deserts, etc. throughout the world
Diet:	Mainly insects; larger spiders may eat mice, lizards, frogs, fish

THE LADYBUG

Phylum:	**Arthropoda** (joint-footed animals)
Class:	**Insecta** (insects)
Order:	**Coleoptera** (sheath-winged)
Size:	Less than ½ inch long
Reproduction:	Four-stage metamorphosis (egg, larva, pupa, adult)
Habitat:	Found in many parts of the world
Diet:	Insects, especially aphids and other plant lice

THE MOLE

Phylum:	**Chordata** (vertebrates)
Class:	**Mammalia** (mammals)
Order:	**Insectivora** (insect-eating)
Size:	5 to 7½ inches including tail
Reproduction:	3 to 7 young per year
Habitat:	Underground burrows in gardens, fields, etc. Found in Europe, Asia and North America
Diet:	Earthworms, insects

THE CAT

Phylum:	**Chordata** (vertebrates)
Class:	**Mammalia** (mammals)
Order:	**Carnivora** (flesh-eating)
Size:	8 to 10 inches tall
Reproduction:	One to three litters of 3 to 5 kittens a year
Habitat:	In vicinity of people. Cats do well in both the city and the country.
Diet:	Rodents (especially mice), small birds

GLOSSARY/INDEX

Annuli   rings or segments, such as those found on the body of the earthworm. (p. 23)

Clutch   a nest of eggs or a group of chicks hatched and cared for at the same time; a brood. (p. 21)

Colonies   large groups of animals that live together and depend on each other for survival. (p. 33)

Elytra   a beetle's front wings, which form a protective shell over the soft hind wings. (p. 27)

Hermaphrodite   an animal or plant having both male and female reproductive organs. (pp. 11, 25)

Hibernate   to spend the winter in a resting or inactive state in which body functions slow down. (p. 29)

Molt   to shed hair, feathers, shells, or other outer layers. (p. 17)

Mucus   a sticky fluid secreted, or given off, by certain animals' bodies to moisten or protect. (p. 12)

Nocturnal   active at night. (p. 43)

Proboscis   a long, flexible straw-like organ. In certain insects, such as flies and butterflies, the proboscis serves as a mouth. (p. 15)

Setae   small, sensitive hairs or bristles such as those found on the underside of the earthworm. (p. 23)

Spinnerets   an organ in spiders and certain insect larvae that produces threads of silk. (p. 40)